WONDERS
OF
NATURE

BY Jane Werner Watson

ILLUSTRATED BY Eloise Wilkin

A GOLDEN BOOK • NEW YORK

Isn't it a wonder
the way the woods know
that spring is coming
before the snow is gone?

The sleeping plants
send up green shoots.
And the tree buds
swell and burst.

Isn't it a wonder
that some seeds
have wings . . .

ASH

ELM

MAPLE

MILKWEED

and some have
tiny silken
parachutes,

DANDELION

and some seeds
are hidden away
in fruits . . .

APPLE

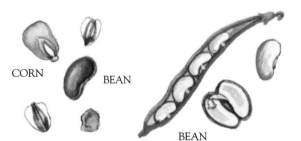

CORN

BEAN

BEAN

and that every seed,
no matter how tiny,
has a whole tiny plant
inside, with food to use
when it starts to grow?

Isn't it a wonder that under the sea there are beautiful, strange gardens where the "flowers" are animals?

SEA GRAPES

SEA ANEMONE

SEA ANEMONE

SEA LILY

SEA URCHIN

SAND DOLLAR

SEA CUCUMBER

Sea anemones,
sea lilies,
sea cucumbers,
and sea grapes—
all are animals!

SEA CUCUMBER

SEA ANEMONE

Isn't it a wonder
that tiny coral animals
under the sea,
which never move,
build great towers
and whole islands
of their tiny shells?

LEAF CORAL

KING CORAL

STAR CORAL

MADREPORE

PURPLE SEA ROD

ORGAN-PIPE
CORAL

BRAIN CORAL

CUP CORAL

Isn't it a wonder
that on the dry desert
some plants have thick stems
in which they store water . . .
and no leaves at all . . .
and lots of prickly spines
to keep thirsty animals
from eating them up?

And the kangaroo rat
who lives on the desert
never drinks water,
but makes it in his body
out of crisp, dry seeds.

Isn't it a wonder
that the beaver
can bite a young tree through
in just a few minutes?

He bites off the branches and uses them
to build a dam across a stream.

And all the birds around,
and the squirrels and opossums,
the deer and the moose,
enjoy that beaver pond.

Isn't it a wonder
that in the jungles
the leaves grow so thickly
overhead that some birds and
animals on the ground
never see the sun?

And there are insects
that look just
like leaves?

And trees start growing
high in the air
on top of other trees,
and send spindly roots down
to the ground?

Isn't it a wonder
that far up north
in the land of ice and snow
we call the arctic,

animals have winter coats
of fur as white as the snow?

Isn't it a wonder that some birds fly
thousands of miles over ocean and land . . .

and return to the same special spots,
to lay their eggs?

That salmon swim
hundreds of miles to shore
and far up the rivers
and over the waterfalls . . .

to return to the same special spots,
to lay their eggs?

Isn't it a wonder
that fireflies
have lights in their bodies
they can flash on and off . . .

that crickets "chirp" by rubbing
their wings?

That some fish
deep in the ocean
have little "electric lights"
dangling in front
of their noses as they swim?

LANTERNFISH

ANGLER

Or little lights
along their sides?

FIREFLY FISH

Isn't it a wonder
that out in the pond
smooth wiggly tadpoles
lose their tails
and grow legs,
and turn into frogs?

And that fuzzy caterpillars
weave silken cocoons
around themselves
and go to sleep,
then wake up as pretty moths
or butterflies?

Isn't it a wonder
that a little baby
that couldn't walk or talk
or feed itself . . .

should grow up to be you?